PINBALL

Navigating Life's Triggers with Strength and Strategy

By DeBorah Lee

Dedicated to my forever PINBALL partner-
Carl L. Lee

Acknowledgment

I want to acknowledge the creators of the game of pinball, for inspiring this life analogy.

Also, I acknowledge Carl L. Lee, who served me unselfishly as a friend and husband, and afforded me the opportunity to play many hours of pinball. It was a weekly activity we enjoyed immensely, and it created a wonderful competitive energy in our relationship, to the point that it didn't matter who won. It was all about the fun. Precious memories - how they linger, gratefully.

Table of Contents

Acknowledgment..iv

Introduction: Insert Coin to Start............................1

Part 1: The 12 Major Triggers 3

    Chapter 1- The Launch 4

    Chapter 2- The Side Hit..13

    Chapter 3- The Tilt Warning 19

    Chapter 4- The Spinning Target 25

    Chapter 5- The Gutter Ball 30

    Chapter 6- The Side Rail.......................................37

    Chapter 7- The Flashing Lights 43

    Chapter 8- The Dead Zone 49

    Chapter 9- The Close Quarters.............................54

    Chapter 10- The Cracked Glass 59

    Chapter 11- Game Over?.......................................64

    Chapter 12- The Endless Loop 69

Part 2: Mastering the Machine 73

    Chapter 13- Knowing Your Flippers.....................74

    Chapter 14- Unlocking the Bonus Round............79

    Chapter 15- The Reset Button 82

Conclusion: Becoming a Pinball Master 85

About the Author 88

Introduction: Insert Coin to Start
Life as a Pinball Machine

Have you ever played Pinball? It's an interesting game. To play, gamers use flippers to launch a metal ball into a playfield filled with targets, ramps, and obstacles, aiming to score points by hitting various features while keeping the ball in play. My hubby and I spent many hours immersed in the enjoyment of it all.

Interestingly, I can see how Life is like a game of pinball - a thrilling and unpredictable challenge, where obstacles appear at every turn, and each decision can send you spiraling in a new direction. Just like a pinball machine, life presents a barrage of triggers: rejection, betrayal, disappointment, and fear, all vying for our attention and threatening to knock us out of the game. Yet, amidst the chaos, an opportunity for growth and resilience lies. Given the right strategies and tools, the hope is that we can beat the odds and win!

In *Pinball: Navigating Life's Triggers with Strength and Strategy*, we dive into the dynamic interplay between life's challenges and the strategies we can adopt to overcome them. As you read, the hope is that you consider your own flippers - those tools, insights, and mindset shifts that help you bounce back from setbacks and power through adversities. How do your flippers help you get past each obstacle? How do you stay afloat?

Each chapter represents a station in this electrifying game of life, where you'll learn how to identify your triggers, build mental strength, and develop a framework for navigating life's tumultuous moments. Through relatable narratives and powerful exemplars, we'll explore what it means to face life's triggers head-on. You'll find practical tools and clearer perspectives designed to arm you with the strategies needed to rise above, ensuring that when life sends you tumbling, you always land on your feet.

Join me on this journey as we flip the script on challenges, changing obstacles into opportunities for enlightenment and growth. Let's get ready to navigate the game of life with renewed strength and a strategic mindset, because every trigger can be a stepping stone, every bump a lesson, and every setback an invitation to spring forward.

Part One

The 12 Major Triggers

Bumpers, Gutters and Obstacles

Chapter 1- The Launch
Triggered by Rejection

The Initial Shot

The game of pinball begins with a launch. With this initial shot, the player forcefully launches a shiny metal ball into the field of play. Here, it interacts with various game elements, including bumpers, flippers, rails, and gutters. This initial trigger sets everything in motion. In the game of life, it mirrors a trigger called rejection.

Rejection often sends us spiraling into motion, emotionally, mentally, and sometimes even spiritually. It's an abrupt force that shakes our confidence, hits our sense of belonging, and throws us into a whirlwind of thoughts:

"Why wasn't I enough?" "What did I do wrong?" "Will I ever be truly accepted?" "Am I not qualified?"

Whether it's being passed over for a job, ghosted by a friend, overlooked by family, or even feeling unseen in our closest relationships, rejection is a trigger that hits hard. It awakens something deep within us, often tied to our earliest experiences of being left out or overlooked. And the more times it happens, the more sensitive we become to even the slightest signs of dismissal.

Rejection doesn't just bruise our egos; it cuts into our identity. It makes us question our value, our voice, and our place in the world. That's why it's not just a minor bump on the playfield of life; it's often the very thing that launches us into cycles of fear, isolation, overcompensation, or people-pleasing.

But here's the truth: rejection does not define you. It may start the motion, but it doesn't have to determine the direction of your life.

.

Flipping Back into Play: Rebuilding Self-Worth and Connection

Flippers are a part of the pinball machine that keeps the ball in play. They're your tools of response, your points of power. And in life, your flippers are your *strategies*, the conscious choices you make to rebuild what rejection tried to destroy. But how do you deploy them effectively?

The first step is reclaiming your self-worth. This isn't about pretending you weren't hurt. It's about acknowledging the pain and choosing not to internalize the lie that rejection means you are less than. Another person's acceptance doesn't assign your worth; it's established by God and reinforced through truth, healing, and intentional self-compassion.

Secondly, connection is key. Rejection often tempts us to withdraw and self-protect. But healing happens in safe, authentic relationships, whether with trusted friends, a support group, a therapist, or a community of faith. True connection reminds us that we're not alone, that we're seen, and that we're still worthy of love and belonging.

Finally, we flip back into play by finding meaning in the moment. What did this rejection teach you? What did it reveal? Sometimes rejection is redirection, an invitation to align with something greater, something truer, something more fitting for who you really are becoming.

So, the next time rejection triggers you, remember: You are not the ball at the mercy of the machine. You are the player, equipped with flippers of strategy and strength. You get to decide what happens next!

Let's reflect on some helpful tools and strategies that you can put into play, starting now.

Reflection Questions: Reclaiming Your Worth

Take a moment to pause and reflect. Let your inner voice rise above the noise of rejection.

1. When was the first time you remember feeling rejected? How did it shape the way you see yourself?

2. What recent rejection still lingers in your thoughts or emotions? Be honest with yourself, where does it hurt the most?

3. In what ways have you responded to rejection in the past (e.g., withdrawing, people-pleasing, striving harder, shutting down)?

Journal Prompt

"Rejection told me I was _____, but God says I am _____. From this moment forward, I choose to believe _____."

Write your truth. Repeat it daily. The initial launch may have been rough, but the game isn't over!

Strategies & Tools for Navigating Rejection

STRATEGY

Name the Wound, Don't Numb It

Avoiding rejection only deepens its grip. Instead of pretending it didn't hurt, acknowledge it out loud (even in writing). Naming your pain is the first step to healing it.

TOOL

Write a *"Truth & Lie" list*, one column for the lies that rejection made you believe, and another for the truth about who you really are. Speak that truth daily.

STRATEGY

Create a Rejection Recovery Routine
Just like a pinball needs to return to its starting point, you need a process that helps you bounce back emotionally and mentally when rejection hits.

TOOL

Create a 3-step routine (e.g., journal → walk → prayer/meditation) to use when facing rejection to keep yourself grounded in your identity, not your pain.

STRATEGY

Don't Chase What God is Removing

Sometimes rejection is divine protection. What feels like loss may be saving you from settling for less than what you're worth.

TOOL

Ask yourself: *"Is this rejection revealing something about what I've been tolerating that doesn't serve me anymore?"*

Write or print scriptures or affirmations about your identity and tape them where you'll see them: mirror, desk, car, phone wallpaper. Let truth reframe your mind daily.

Chapter 2- The Side Hit
Triggered by Betrayal

The Hit You Didn't See Coming

In a pinball game, it's often the side bumpers that catch you off guard. One second, you're gaining momentum, the next you're ricocheting in a direction you didn't plan for. Betrayal hits just as suddenly, jarringly, and disorientingly. It is more than just disappointment; it's the wound that comes when someone you trusted breaks the agreement of safety, loyalty, or love. Whether it's a friend who shares your secrets, a spouse who breaks their vows, a mentor who misleads, or a leader who lets you down, it cuts deep. You think, "I didn't see that coming." "How could they?" "I gave them my trust, and they used it against me." The emotional impact of betrayal often leads to confusion, anger, shame, and a profound sense of loss. The loss is not just of the relationship, but of your innocence, your security, and sometimes, your ability to trust again. So, how do you move on?

Let's dive into some tools to help you do just that!

Reflection Questions:
Reclaiming Trust After Betrayal

1. Who betrayed you, and what did that betrayal take from you?

2. What are you still carrying because of that experience?

3. What have you learned about trust, and what needs to be healed before you can offer it again?

Journal Prompt

"The betrayal hurt me deeply. But it also taught me
_____. *From here, I choose to* _____.*"*

Breathe…Take your time and write how you feel in this moment

_____
_____
_____
_____
_____
_____
_____
_____
_____
_____
_____
_____
_____
_____
_____

Strategies & Tools for Navigating Betrayal

♟ STRATEGY

Betrayal includes a form of relational grief. Give yourself permission to mourn, not just the person, but what you thought you had.

🔨 TOOL

Create a ritual for release, burn a letter, speak aloud what you're letting go of, or write a goodbye note to the version of the relationship you thought was real.

♟ STRATEGY

Forgiveness and reconciliation are not the same. You can choose healing while also choosing distance. Healthy boundaries are the flippers that keep you from falling into resentment.

🔨 TOOL

List three boundaries you need going forward: emotionally, spiritually, or practically.

🏰 STRATEGY

Betrayal doesn't mean you can never trust again, but you may need to retrain your ability to discern and rebuild.

🔨 TOOL

Start with low-risk relationships. Practice small trust-building exercises, such as sharing your feelings, asking for support, and allowing yourself to be seen, bit by bit.

Chapter 3- The Tilt Warning
Triggered by Unjust Treatment

When Life Tilts and the System Fails You

Are you enjoying learning about pinball? Let's continue. In this game, a "tilt" happens when the player shakes or nudges the machine too hard, causing it to freeze and end the game. It's a built-in defense mechanism because too much force causes the system to shut down. For many of us, unjust treatment triggers that same internal "tilt." The injustice overwhelms us, the emotional pressure builds, and eventually... we shut down.

Unjust treatment is one of the most disorienting triggers because it strikes at the core of our belief that the world, or at least certain people, should be fair. Whether it's being blamed for something you didn't do, overlooked because of bias, mistreated by authority, or judged unfairly - it can leave you emotionally frozen.

The danger? If not processed, unjust treatment can lead to chronic resentment, internalized shame, or a belief that you must overperform just to be seen. Feel free to use the following tools to assist you in this needed processing.

Reflection Questions:
Rebalancing After Injustice

1. What injustice have you experienced that still feels unresolved?

2. What did that moment teach you about power, voice, and visibility?

3. How has it impacted your view of yourself, and how can you reclaim your truth?

Journal Prompt

"I was treated unfairly when _____, but I am not de-
fined by that. I choose to _____ in response to what
happened."

_____

_____

_____

_____

_____

_____

_____

_____

_____

_____

_____

_____

_____

Strategies and Tools for Processing Injustice

♟♜ STRATEGY

Acknowledge the Imbalance

Denial keeps the system tilted. You don't have to justify what happened. Name it. Call it what it was: unfair, untrue, unkind.

⚒ TOOL

Write a short "justice statement" that honors your experience.

"It wasn't fair that _____. That treatment didn't reflect my worth or my truth."

STRATEGY

Channel the Pain into Purpose

You don't need to "get over it", you get to grow through it. Righteous anger can become fuel for advocacy, creativity, or change.

TOOL

Ask: *"How can I turn this pain into purpose?"* It might be mentoring, writing, speaking out, or creating something redemptive.

Chapter 4- The Spinning Target
Triggered by Challenged Beliefs

When Life Hits What You Thought Was Solid

What happens when the foundations of our lives are shaken? When our beliefs confront the trials of life, the words of others, or the truths hidden within ourselves?

Let's look to our pinball game for insights. In the pinball game of life, belief bumpers are like those sturdy targets that the ball bounces off repeatedly, creating sound, light, and energy. They represent our internal framework: our core beliefs; what we believe about ourselves, others,

God, the world, and what's possible. But what happens when those bumpers get hit too hard... and don't bounce back? Maybe you grew up believing "If I do good, then good will come back to me." Or "God will always protect me from harm." Or "People are generally trustworthy." Then life happened! A loved one transitioned. You were betrayed. Your prayers went unanswered.

Suddenly, what you believed no longer *matches* what you're experiencing. And it hurts. Challenged beliefs can trigger deep internal conflict, confusion, disillusionment, and even a crisis of faith or identity. But here's the truth: challenged beliefs are not always a sign of weakness. Conversely, they can be an invitation to grow deeper.

I invite you to use the following reflections to usher you into deeper growth.

.

Reflection Questions:
When Beliefs Get Shaken

1. What core belief has been challenged in your life?

2. How has that shift impacted your relationship with God, others, or yourself?

3. What new truth or deeper understanding might be forming through this?

_____

_____

_____

_____

_____

_____

_____

Journal Prompt

"The belief that was challenged was _____. Now, I'm learning to believe _____."

_____

_____

_____

_____

_____

_____

_____

_____

_____

_____

_____

_____

_____

_____

_____

_____

_____

Strategies and Tools for Navigating Challenged Beliefs

♜ STRATEGY

Identify the Cracked Belief

Start by naming the belief that got challenged. What felt solid... until it wasn't?

⚒ TOOL

Finish this sentence: *"I used to believe* _____, *but then* _____*."*

♜ STRATEGY

Grieve the Shift

Belief changes can feel like a death. It's okay to mourn what you used to hold onto, even if you're gaining something more grounded in return.

⚒ TOOL

Create a "belief timeline" to reflect on how your core truths have evolved. Remember to give yourself permission to feel.

Chapter 5- The Gutter Ball
Triggered by Helplessness or Loss of Control

The Frenzy of Losing Control

Have you ever felt like your life is spinning out of control? What happens when helplessness creeps in and shakes your sense of agency? Are you ready to acknowledge those unsettling moments that challenge your peace and leave you questioning your ability to navigate your own life? Are you ready to explore how to regain your grip?

In pinball, the spinner is a fast-moving part of the play-field that makes the ball fly wildly when it passes through. The ball spins in every direction, unpredictable, chaotic, and hard to follow. That's what helplessness feels like: you're moving, but you're not the one steering.

Loss of control is one of the most common and disorienting emotional triggers. It can occur during unexpected illnesses, job loss, natural disasters, financial crises, or family chaos, which reminds us that we aren't in charge. For those who value order or predictability, it can be especially painful. Here's the good news: I believe triggers are created for awareness, not downfall. (*More on this in part two! Stay tuned.*)

When helplessness overtakes you, you might freeze, try to over-control, or shut down entirely. Either way, the internal chaos begins to mirror the external one. But even in those moments, you still have power, the power to anchor yourself, even when you can't stop the spin. I'm sure practical tips for navigating this frenzy are welcomed. So, let's drop some anchors, shall we?

Reflection Questions:
Anchoring in the Spin

1. When was the last time you felt completely out of control? What triggered it?
2. How do you usually respond: freeze, fight, flight, or over-function?
3. What might it look like to accept the chaos *without* letting it consume you?

Journal Prompt

"Even though I can't control _____, I still have access to the power to _____. I choose to anchor myself in _____."

_____

_____

_____

_____

_____

_____

_____

_____

_____

_____

_____

_____

_____

_____

Strategies & Tools for Regaining Grounding: Slowing the Spin

STRATEGY

Identify One Area You *Can* Influence
Even if it's small - your breath, your reaction, your routine. You need something to hold on to when everything feels like it's slipping.

TOOL

Create a "Circle of Control" diagram:
- Inside: what you can do, think, or influence
- Outside: what's not yours to carry

Focus on what's inside.

STRATEGY

Practice Grounding Techniques

When your thoughts are spinning, your body can be your anchor.

TOOL

Try the 5-4-3-2-1 Grounding Method:
- 5 things you see
- 4 things you can touch
- 3 things you hear
- 2 things you smell
- 1 thing you can taste

Or use breathwork: inhale for 4 seconds, hold for 4 seconds, exhale for 6 seconds.

♜ STRATEGY

Release the Illusion of Total Control

Surrender isn't defeat, it's wisdom. Accepting what's not in your hands gives you the freedom to focus on what is.

⚒ TOOL

Prayer or meditation: *"God, help me release what is not mine to carry. Give me peace in what I can't predict and strength in what I can choose."*

RAILS

Chapter 6- The Side Rail
Triggered by Exclusion or Being Ignored

When You're Left on the Sidelines

Now, let's strike at the heart of belonging, visibility, and the pain of being overlooked. In the pinball machine of life, there are moments when you feel like the ball *never even touched the playfield*. You're not in the game. You're on the side, forgotten, ignored, excluded. And while it may not feel as jarring as rejection, it cuts just as deep. Being excluded or ignored activates primal fears: *Do I matter? Do they see me? Why wasn't I chosen?* Whether it happens in your family, social circles, workplace, or church, this trigger makes you question your worth and can lead to self-doubt, loneliness, or isolation.

But being "out of bounds" doesn't mean you're without purpose. Sometimes, those very moments are divine redirections, spaces to clarify identity apart from applause, and to heal the wounds of invisibility.

This "internal" work can be the most difficult and require the most guidance. I got you! Try these reflective strategies to help heal the wounds you didn't know existed.

Reflection Questions
Healing the Wound of Being Left Out

1. Where in your life have you felt excluded or ignored? How did it shape your self-view?
2. What spaces affirm your voice and presence?
3. What might God be showing or preserving in the "not being included"?

Journal Prompt

"Being left out made me feel _____, but now I choose to believe _____. I am seen, valued, and _____."

_____

_____

_____

_____

_____

_____

_____

_____

_____

_____

_____

_____

_____

_____

_____

_____

Reclaiming Visibility: Strategies to Overcome the Sting of Exclusion

♟ **STRATEGY**

Validate your emotions without letting them lead.
Being left out hurts. Period! Allow yourself to feel it, but don't let it define you.

🔨 **TOOL:**

Try emotion labeling: *"This feels like sadness and disappointment, not truth about my value."*

♟ **STRATEGY**

Create Space Where You're Seen
Find or build communities where your voice matters. That might mean leaning into safe friendships, seeking professional support, or creating a space where others like you feel at home.

TOOL:

> ➤ Community Audit: List places/people where you feel seen and those where you feel invisible. Where do you need to lean in, or step away?

> ➤ Reframe the "No" as Protection or Preparation. Sometimes being left out is painful *and* protective. It may be God's way of making room for your "yes" elsewhere.

AFFIRMATION:

"I am not forgotten. I am being positioned. Where I'm unseen by man, I'm held in the hands of God."

Chapter 7- The Flashing Lights
Triggered by Disapproval or Criticism

When Approval Becomes Addictive

In a pinball machine, flashing lights are everywhere. They are bright, bold, and loud. They're designed to grab your attention, signaling something exciting, rewarding, or urgent. But not every light means success. Some just distract or mislead, throwing off your focus and pulling your eyes away from what really matters: the ball in play.

In life, those flashing lights show up as the constant need for approval, the anxiety of being judged, and the sting of criticism. They demand your emotional attention, disrupt your internal rhythm, and make you doubt your worth.

Just like in pinball, the more you chase every flashing light, the more you risk losing sight of your true aim. Disapproval and criticism can feel blinding, especially when you've tied your value to others' applause. But you were never meant to be powered by the flickers of fleeting affirmation. Your steadiness comes not from being liked, but from being grounded. When you root your identity in truth rather than perception, disapproval ceases to be a danger, and criticism becomes a tool, not a trigger.

You know the drill- let's combat this trigger with truth!

Reflection Questions:

1. What recent criticism has lingered in your thoughts? Was it constructive, or did it hit an old wound?

2. How do you typically respond to disapproval, defensively, passively, or reflectively?

3. What truth about your identity can anchor you when facing harsh or unfair criticism?

Journal Prompt:

"Criticism makes me feel _____, but I know that I am still _____. I will learn to grow, not shut down."

_____

_____

_____

_____

_____

_____

_____

_____

_____

_____

_____

_____

_____

_____

_____

Strategies and Tools for Navigating Criticism

♟♜ STRATEGY

Pause Before Processing

When criticism or disapproval comes, resist the urge to react immediately. Take a moment to breathe, step back, and ask yourself: Is this about me, or is it about them? Creating space allows your nervous system to regulate and your logic to engage.

Identity Anchoring Practice

Each week, revisit a core list of your strengths, values, and non-negotiables. This strategy reinforces a stable self-image and helps you recover faster when external feedback attempts to distort your sense of self.

⚒ TOOL

Mirror Work with Truth Statements

Stand in front of a mirror daily and speak affirming truths over yourself (e.g., *"I am not defined by approval; I am already accepted and enough."*).

This practice helps rewire your self-perception and anchor your value internally rather than externally.

Criticism Filter Worksheet

Create a simple two-column worksheet labeled: "Constructive" and "Destructive." When you receive criticism, sort it through this filter. If it's constructive, reflect and grow. If it's destructive, release it without internalizing it. This tool builds emotional resilience and healthy boundaries.

AFFIRMATION:

"I can grow from feedback without shrinking in value."

=

Chapter 8- The Dead Zone
Triggered by Feeling Unwanted or Unneeded

When You Wonder If You Matter

A ball slipping through the flippers and down the drain is one of the most frustrating moments in pinball. It's not explosive, it's quiet. That's how this trigger often feels: *a subtle ache of invisibility.*

This emotional wound often stems from abandonment, unmet needs, or seasons where others simply weren't present. The lie it whispers is: *"You're not necessary. You're just... extra, expendable."*

There's a quiet ache that comes with being unseen, not just physically, but emotionally and spiritually. It's the sting of giving your all and still feeling like wallpaper in the room. You are present but easily missed. You may laugh, smile, serve, and show up, yet deep inside, you're asking, *"Does anyone notice me? Do I even matter here?"*

The next tools are so vital because they will remind you that just because you were overlooked, it doesn't mean you are unworthy. Your presence is powerful, even when it goes unnoticed.

Reflection Questions

1. When have you felt most invisible or emotionally overlooked in your relationships?
2. How have those feelings shaped the way you engage or disengage with others?
3. What new beliefs about your worth and presence are you prepared to accept?

Journal Prompt:

"When I feel unwanted, I remind myself that my worth is not based on usefulness but on my existence. I am _____, and I still have purpose."

_____

_____

_____

_____

_____

_____

_____

_____

_____

_____

_____

_____

_____

_____

_____

Tools for Reclaiming Value and Purpose

➢ Inventory Your Impact
Journal moments when your presence made a difference. Don't minimize them.

➢ Redefine What "Needed" Means
Your value isn't transactional. You don't have to "earn" belonging.

➢ Seek Purpose, Not Just Placement
Ask God: *Where am I meant to pour out? Who needs what I carry?*

AFFIRMATION:

"Even when I feel unseen, I am still significant, my presence carries purpose and value."

Chapter 9- The Close Quarters
Triggered by Feeling Smothered or Too Needed

When Everyone Needs Something, All at Once

Multi-ball mode in pinball is thrilling but chaotic. It's marked by multiple balls flying, multiple goals, and very little control. That's how this trigger feels: *everyone wants something from you, and there's nothing left to give.*

This is especially common among caregivers, leaders, parents, and those who provide assistance. The trigger emerges when boundaries are blurry, and burnout is near.

There's an unspoken pressure that builds when you're constantly the go-to person or the one who shows up, holds it together, and keeps everything afloat. At first, it feels noble, even affirming. But over time, it can start to feel like you're being swallowed whole. When your identity becomes wrapped up in being needed, it's easy to lose sight of your own needs and your own space to breathe.

Boundaries become blurred, and burnout becomes inevitable. Setting limits and saying no doesn't mean you love others any less; it means you're finally loving yourself enough to recognize when the load is too heavy. You have a right to step back, to exhale, and to reclaim the pieces of yourself that got buried beneath everyone else's expectations. Setting appropriate boundaries will be one of the greatest gifts that you can give yourself. Let's work!

Reflection Questions

1. Do you ever feel emotionally crowded or overly depended on? In which relationships?
2. How do you set or struggle to maintain healthy emotional boundaries?
3. What's one step you can take this week to reclaim balance without guilt?

Journal Prompt:

"I am allowed to protect my peace by limiting _____.
Even if others don't understand _____, I choose to
honor my limits."

_____

_____

_____

_____

_____

_____

_____

_____

_____

_____

_____

_____

_____

_____

Tools for Overcoming Overwhelm: Boundaries

1. Establish Non-Negotiables: Protect time, space and silence as sacred.
2. Differentiate Between Urgency and Importance. Not everything that's urgent is essential.
3. Learn to Say No Without Guilt: Saying no to others can be saying yes to your own health.

AFFIRMATION

"I am allowed to set boundaries without guilt. Caring for others does not require me to abandon myself."

Chapter 10- The Cracked Glass
Triggered by Insecurity

Seeing Through a Broken Lens

A cracked pinball machine glass makes the whole game harder to follow. Insecurity works the same way. It distorts how we see ourselves and how we interpret others' actions. This trigger often masks itself behind overachievement, comparison, or perfectionism. At its core, it's about fear of not being "enough."

The fear of *not being enough* is a deep and often quiet wound. It whispers lies that say you're too much and not enough all at once. Such a contradiction. It says you are not smart enough, attractive enough, spiritual enough, or worthy enough. This fear often takes root in early experiences of comparison, neglect, or conditional acceptance and grows into a lens through which you view every relationship, opportunity, and challenge. It causes you to shrink when you should shine and question your worth, even when you're overqualified. Insecurity convinces you to settle, to silence yourself, to second-guess every instinct. But here's the truth: those feelings are not fixed facts; rather, they are distortions. And while cracked glass can distort the view, it doesn't make the object behind it any less real or valuable.

Strategic tools are definitely needed for this one! The hope is that the following will help you see yourself more clearly, challenge those internal distortions, and rebuild your confidence from the inside out. Are you ready to keep diving? Let's work.

Reflection Questions

1. What are the loudest insecurities you currently carry, and where did they begin?

2. How have these insecurities shaped your choices or held you back?

3. What affirming truth or Scripture can replace one recurring insecure thought?

_____

_____

_____

_____

_____

_____

_____

_____

_____

_____

_____

_____

_____

_____

_____

Journal Prompt:

"Insecurity says _____. But truth says I am _____.
I choose to believe the truth today."

_____

_____

_____

_____

_____

_____

_____

_____

_____

_____

_____

_____

_____

Tools for Overcoming Self-Doubt

1. Challenge the Inner Critic: Replace "I'm not good enough" with "I'm learning and growing."
2. Stop the Comparison Spiral: You are not behind. You are on your own timeline.
3. Speak Truth Daily: Create personalized affirmations grounded in Scripture.

AFFIRMATION

"I am not defined by doubt, I am growing into confidence and truth. I choose to see myself through the lens of grace, not fear."

Chapter 11- Game Over?
Triggered by Loss of Independence

The Humility of Needing Help

Having to rely on others can be challenging. It may evoke shame, fear, or anger. However, reliance isn't a sign of weakness; it often opens the door to deeper connection and spiritual surrender.

In pinball, when the game ends, the ball comes to rest, and there is no further movement or control. That's what this trigger can feel like: losing mobility, income, autonomy, or the ability to "handle it on your own."

Admitting you need help can feel like surrendering a badge of strength, especially if you've been praised for your resilience or conditioned to equate independence with value. However, the truth is that it takes far more humility and courage to reach out than it does to pretend everything is okay. Needing help doesn't make you weak; it makes you *human*. We were never meant to carry the weight of life alone. Recognizing when you're emotionally or spiritually depleted is not a flaw; it's wisdom.

Use the following strategies to help you reframe the value of "Help", and starting today, embrace it when needed!

Reflection Questions

1. In what area of life do you feel a tension between needing help and wanting autonomy?
2. How does your relationship with control affect your peace or anxiety levels?
3. Where might God be inviting you to trust Him more, even if it means letting go?

Tools for Navigating the Loss of Independence

STRATEGY

Reframe the Role: Shift from "Doing" to "Being"

When your identity is rooted in what you can do, losing independence feels like losing a part of yourself. But your worth is not in your productivity; it's in your presence, your wisdom, and your essence.

TOOL

Create a "Being List" instead of a to-do list. Write: *"To-day, I choose to be..."* (peaceful, present, grateful, valuable, creative, etc.) This re-centers your day around who you are, not just what you accomplish.

STRATEGY

Establish Interdependence, Not Dependence

There is a difference between healthy interdependence and helplessness. Letting others help doesn't make you weak; it makes you human. And God often uses others as the answer to our prayers.

TOOL

Practice asking for help in one small area each day. Journal how it felt, what you learned, and what connections were strengthened as a result.

AFFIRMATION

"Even when I need help, I am not helpless. My value is not in what I do, but in who I am."

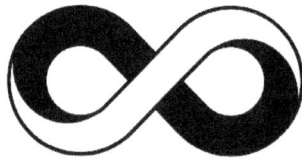

Chapter 12- The Endless Loop
Triggered by the Fear of Failure

Nothing is more paralyzing than the fear of failure. In a pinball game, there are times when the ball seems to bounce back and forth between the same two bumpers, over and over. No progress. No points. Just noise and repetition. This is the endless loop - and in life, it often mirrors the paralyzing cycle of perfectionism fueled by the fear of failure.

When the fear of failing triggers you, you can get stuck trying to perfect every detail, overanalyzing every move, and avoiding risk at all costs. The pressure to get it right can be suffocating. Ironically, this need for perfection *prevents progress*, keeping you stuck in a replay mode, both mentally and emotionally.

But failure isn't the enemy, *it's the teacher.* The true "high score" in life comes when we stop seeing failure as the end, and start recognizing it as *feedback.* When we reframe failure as part of growth, we unlock courage, creativity, and freedom. The following tools are sure to help.

Reflection Questions

1. What failure in your past still echoes in your decisions today?

2. How do you define success, and has that definition changed as you've healed?

3. What risk or leap are you currently resisting because of fear?

_____

_____

_____

_____

_____

_____

_____

_____

_____

_____

_____

_____

_____

_____

Tools for Navigating Fear of Failure:

- Shift your definition of failure: It's not falling down, it's refusing to get back up.
- Practice "progress over perfection": Set goals based on movement, not mastery.
- Expose the Fear: Journal what you're afraid will happen if you fail, and challenge its truth.
- Try and Reflect: After each attempt, ask: "What did I learn?" not "Did I win?"
- Use Scripture as an anchor: "Though the righteous fall seven times, they rise again…" (Proverbs 24:16)

Letting go of perfection opens the door to possibility. Your worth is not based on flawless performance, but on your faithful pursuit. Fear of failure loses its grip when you give yourself permission to learn and begin again.

AFFIRMATION

"Failure is not my finish line; it's a stepping stone to growth. I am free to try, learn, and rise again."

Part Two

Mastering the Machine

Tools and Strategies for Lasting Strength

Chapter 13- Knowing Your Flippers
Emotional Regulation and Self-Awareness

Let's talk about control. We all feel better when we have it, right? In pinball, your flippers are your only real control. You can't stop the ball from being launched. You can't remove the bumpers, gutters, or obstacles. But you can *learn to respond*. You can flip with timing, accuracy, and skill, if you're paying attention.

In life, *your emotional regulation tools equate to your flippers*. These are the mental, spiritual, and physical strategies you use to regain balance when life hits you unexpectedly. And it will! But here's the key: regulation doesn't happen in a vacuum. It requires something essential beforehand. That key is self-awareness.

Think of self-awareness as the internal *training ground*. It is the moment when you become aware of what's happening inside you before you respond externally. It's being able to say, "I'm not just angry, I also feel disrespected," or "I'm not shut down, I feel overwhelmed and unheard." This level of internal honesty prepares you to engage your emotional flippers with purpose, not panic.

Without self-awareness, emotional regulation is like flipping blindly, hoping to hit something that works. But when you're self-aware, you can *see the ball*, *read the momentum*, and *make intentional moves* to stay in play. Self-awareness involves:

- Recognizing your patterns under stress
- Naming your emotions as they arise
- Understanding your triggers and why they exist
- Observing your body's signals (tight jaw, racing heart, shallow breathing)

Once you're aware, you're no longer at the mercy of your reactions. Now, you can choose your response.

Triggers Are Not the Enemy; They're Indicators

A powerful shift in emotional health happens when you stop seeing triggers as threats and start seeing them as *information*. Triggers are not inherently negative. They are alerts and invitations to pay attention. They let you know something under the surface is being activated. When you treat a trigger like an enemy, you either fight it or flee from it. But when you treat it like a messenger, you can pause and ask:

- "What is this showing me?"
- "Where did this start?"
- "What do I need in this moment?"

This changes everything!

Being triggered doesn't mean you're weak. It means you're alive, and something inside you still needs to be seen, healed, or honored. Your triggers don't disqualify you. Instead, they *guide* you. When you understand them, you can respond to life with wisdom rather than reaction. That's how you become emotionally agile. That's how you self-regulate. That's how you stay in play.

Strategies and Tools for Emotional Regulation & Self-Awareness

♜♟ STRATEGIES

> Check Your Internal Scoreboard

Before reacting, pause and assess what you're actually feeling. Are you angry or embarrassed? Are you anxious, or overstimulated? Emotions are information. When you learn to decode them, you're less likely to misfire.

Practice daily emotional check-ins. Ask:
- What am I feeling?
- Why might I be feeling it?
- What do I need right now?

> Slow the Ball Down

Just like a pinball slows with a nudge of the flipper, you can interrupt an emotional spiral with intentional calming techniques.

Use the *Name–Breathe–Choose* method:
- Name the emotion
- Breathe deeply for 30 seconds

- Choose a response that aligns with your values (not just your feelings)

➢ Build Your Personal Flipper Kit
Every emotionally aware person has a go-to toolkit. Yours may include prayer, a walk, journaling, or calling a friend.

Make a list of 5–7 emotional reset practices and keep it visible. Practice *proactive* regulation, not just reactive survival.

⚒ TOOLS for Managing Reactions:

- Body scan: Notice where tension builds (jaw, shoulders, chest) and release it consciously.
- Prayer and breathwork: Invite the Holy Spirit into your regulation. Ask: "Lord, help me see this clearly."
- Therapy and accountability: Don't do the inner work alone; wise counsel gives perspective.

Chapter 14- Unlocking the Bonus Round
Cultivating Resilience

We have almost completed the pinball game. Next up is the bonus round. Here is where all your earlier plays add up. It's the overflow. It's the extra opportunity. It's the bonus! In life, resilience unlocks your bonus rounds.

Resilience isn't about denying pain. It's about refusing to let pain define you. Every time you bounce back after betrayal, or breathe through the weight of rejection, or rebuild after being broken, you're scoring points. You're learning. You're growing. The key is this: resilience isn't just born from strength. It's born from struggle. The more intentional you are about learning from your challenges, the more equipped you become for what lies ahead.

Strategies to Build Resilience:

- **Reframe Adversity:**
  Ask, "What is this here to teach me?"
- **Track Patterns:** Journal triggers and responses to identify what's working and what's not.
- **Celebrate Small Wins:** Every bounce-back moment is a sign of progress.
- **Connect to Purpose:** Your pain is a classroom. Don't leave without the lesson.
- **Anchor in Scripture:** "We are hard pressed on every side... but not crushed." (2 Corinthians 4:8)

TOOLS

➢ Build a "Resilience Resume"

Sometimes we forget how far we've already come. Creating a tangible list of what you've overcome helps you shift from "I can't" to "I already have."

List five moments in your life when you bounced back from hardship. Write what the challenge was, what you learned, and how you grew.

➤ Establish a Recovery Routine

Resilient people don't just "push through"; they recover intentionally. Rest is not weakness; it's wisdom.

Create a post-trigger care plan with 3 categories:

- *What I'll do physically* (e.g., sleep, hydration, movement)
- *What I'll do emotionally* (e.g., journal, cry, talk)
- *What I'll do spiritually* (e.g., pray, meditate, worship)

➤ Anchor in a Scripture or Statement

Resilience often requires a repeatable truth, something you declare over yourself when your strength is shaken.
Choose a scripture or phrase like:

- *"This is hard, but I am not hopeless."*
- *"God is my refuge and strength..."* (Psalm 46:1)
  Recite it daily, or write it where you'll see it often.

Chapter 15- The Reset Button
Embracing Grace and New Beginnings

In life and pinball, sometimes we lose the ball. We misfire, we miss the target, and we watch everything we've built drain away. But the beauty of God's grace is that there's *always a reset button.* Shame says, "It's Over." Grace says, "Let's begin again!" Self-compassion is the holy permission to reset, not in denial, but in truth.

Letting go doesn't mean forgetting what happened. It means releasing the weight of carrying it as your identity. Forgiveness of others and yourself isn't a one-time act. It's a lifestyle of freedom. Easier said than done? Maybe not. Here are some suggestions that are sure to help.

STRATEGIES

➢ Separate Who You Are from What You Did

Shame says, "You are your mistake." Grace says, "You are more than your worst moment." To move forward, you must detach your identity from your actions.

Write a two-column list:

- Left side: What happened or what you did.
- Right side: What it does NOT mean about your identity.

  For example: *"I failed a relationship" ≠ "I am un-lovable."*

➢ Use the Grace Mirror Daily

We often judge ourselves by a harsher standard than we use for others. Practicing self-compassion begins by seeing yourself the way God sees you.

Each morning, look in the mirror and speak this aloud: *"I am forgiven. I am growing. I am not disqualified."*

You can also write a grace statement and place it on your bathroom mirror, phone lock screen, or journal.

➤ Declare the Reset and Begin Again

You don't need a new year or a big breakthrough to start over; you need a decision. Each day offers a fresh start.

Start each day with a *reset ritual,* such as:

- Breathing prayer (e.g., inhale: *"New mercy,"* exhale: *"Fresh start."*)
- Writing "I begin again today" at the top of your planner or journal
- Reading Lamentations 3:22–23: *"His mercies are new every morning…"*

⚒ TOOLS

- Daily reset prayer: "God, I release what I can't fix. Renew what I can."
- Shame Inventory: List the areas where shame is still speaking. Challenge each with grace.
- Practice radical self-forgiveness: Speak to yourself like someone you love.
- Forgive others to free yourself: Unforgiveness is a pinball stuck in place.
- Claim your next move: You can start again, today.

Conclusion: Becoming a Pinball Master
Thriving Beyond the Triggers

There will be times when life feels like chaos. You will experience one emotional collision after another. In fact, you may have entered this book feeling out of control, frustrated, or stuck. But by now, the hope is that you've discovered something deeper: being triggered doesn't mean you're broken, it means you're human; it means you're *healing*. The hope is that this book has provided insight and tools for surviving the game when it doesn't feel like much fun.

As you continue your journey through the wild mechanics of your emotions, you will face the sharp sting of rejection, the ache of being overlooked, the pressure of perfection, and the shame that says, *"This is the end."* But you will survive! And you won't just survive, you'll strategize. You will learn the rules of the game, recognize the traps, anticipate the bumpers, and, most importantly, flip *with power*. You will triumph over what once trapped you.

That's the mark of a *Pinball Master.*

A Pinball Master isn't someone who avoids being triggered. Instead, it's someone who has learned how to navigate their emotional world with wisdom, courage, and grace. It's the person who knows that life will press in, but they won't collapse. They'll *bounce back*. Not by pretending everything is fine, but by learning how to play smarter, respond softer, and rise stronger.

And here's the truth: you were never meant to stay in the machine. You were made to rise above it.

You've got the flippers. You've got the playbook. You've faced the drain and still found grace.

So now, walk into your next season as a Pinball Master. Own your triggers without shame. Use your tools with confidence. Live with open hands, a soft heart, and sharp wisdom. And when life tries to send you spiraling again, and it will - you know what to do:

Breathe.
Pray.
Flip back into play.

This isn't game over.
It's just the beginning of a higher score.
Keep playing with strategy.

Keep rising with strength.

And never forget…

You are the master of your response.
And with God's help, you will always bounce back.

With Compassion and Faith,

DeBorah Lee

About the Author

DeBorah Lee is a distinguished Christian psychotherapist and coach. She is a beacon of empowerment who guides women on a journey toward self-discovery, resilience, and authentic living. With an unwavering commitment, DeBorah instills in women the power to assert their worth, embolden their spirits, and cultivate relationships that harmonize with their aspirations and values.

A trailblazer in the realms of psychology and coaching, her professional trajectory is nothing short of remarkable. As a Licensed Professional Counselor and Licensed Clinical Alcohol and Drug Counselor, she has ventured across diverse arenas, amassing wisdom and insight that have uniquely positioned her to transform lives. Her experiences span the educational landscape, where she has left indelible imprints as a mentor and guide to students of all ages. Her roles as a dedicated guidance counselor and educator have enriched young minds and catalyzed her passion for fostering growth and resilience.

Beyond the classroom, DeBorah's journey has threaded through the fabric of various domains. She has poured her wisdom and experience into teen pregnancy programs, young women's group homes, halfway houses, outpatient facilities, and residential programs, has served as Coordinator of Displaced Homemakers, training women to re-enter the workforce, and has played an instrumental role as the Director of Patient and Family Services for the American Cancer Society. She has also worked with young men as the Director/Educator of a program aimed at reducing the retention rate of middle school boys who fail to advance to high school. DeBorah has consistently championed the well-being of individuals and families in all realms of service, with an overwhelming dedication to guiding others on the path toward self-sufficiency.

DeBorah Lee's influence is truly multifaceted. A luminary within the spiritual realm, her leadership roles across every facet of church life have left an indelible mark on congregations worldwide. The resounding impact of her monthly Pep Talks for Women continues to resonate across generations, igniting empowerment and transformation. Her legacy expands through women's conferences, captivating keynote speeches, and the establishment of Comrades USA, a testament to her tireless efforts to foster unity and empowerment.

Her commitment to spreading her message of empowerment knows no bounds. As a globe-trotter for the gospel, DeBorah has traversed the United States, journeyed through the profound landscapes of Israel, and shared her wisdom in the heart of China.

Amidst her achievements, DeBorah Lee holds dear her most cherished role: that of a devoted mother to a son, a loving daughter-in-love, and a cherished "MeMa" to four treasured grandchildren. Her personal life seamlessly intertwines with her professional endeavors, painting a picture of a woman who embodies the principles she imparts.

DeBorah Lee's story is one of resilience, empowerment, unwavering faith, and a deep-seated commitment to fostering positive change. With an illustrious career that has spanned a spectrum of roles, she continues to stand as a symbol of unwavering strength, guidance, and confidence for women across the globe. Through her wisdom, countless lives have been touched, transformed, and empowered to embark on their own journeys toward authenticity and fulfillment.

WOMEN
of wisdom and poise

GROUP COACHING PROGRAM

- Bi-Weekly Meetings Exploring the Complexities of Womanhood
- Accountability Coaching
- Interactive Q & A and Discussion
- Elite Community of Women
- Discounts on Master Classes

COACH
DEBORAH LEE

JOIN NOW

www.iamdeborahlee.com

www.ingramcontent.com/pod-product-compliance
Lightning Source LLC
Chambersburg PA
CBHW060403050426
42449CB00009B/1879